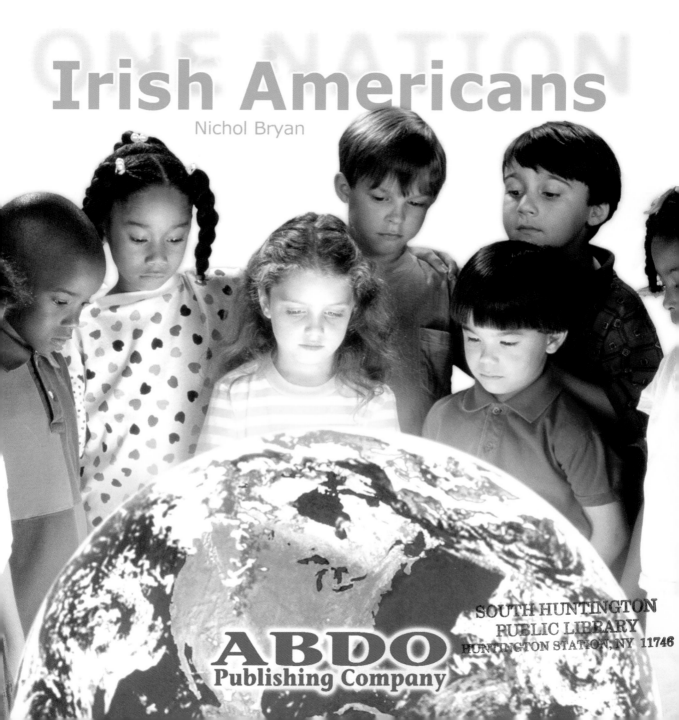

ONE NATION

Irish Americans

Nichol Bryan

ABDO
Publishing Company

visit us at
www.abdopub.com

Published by ABDO Publishing Company, 4940 Viking Drive, Edina, Minnesota 55435.
Copyright © 2004 by Abdo Consulting Group, Inc. International copyrights reserved in all
countries. No part of this book may be reproduced in any form without written permission from
the publisher.

Printed in the United States.

Cover Photo: The Sexton Company
Interior Photos: AP/Wide World p. 21; Corbis pp. 1, 2-3, 4-5, 6, 7, 8, 9, 10, 11, 12, 14, 16, 23,
    25, 26, 27, 29, 30-31; Kayte Deioma p. 22; The Sexton Company pp. 19, 20

Series Coordinator: Jennifer R. Krueger
Editors: Kristianne E. Buechler, Kate A. Conley
Art Direction & Maps: Neil Klinepier

All of the U.S. population statistics in the One Nation series are taken from the 2000 Census.

Library of Congress Cataloging-in-Publication Data

Bryan, Nichol, 1958-
    Irish Americans / Nichol Bryan.
        p. cm. -- (One nation)
    Includes index.
    Summary: Provides information on the history of Ireland and on the customs, language,
religion, and experiences of Irish Americans.
    ISBN 1-59197-528-X
        1. Irish Americans--Juvenile literature. [1. Irish Americans. 2. Immigrants.] I. Title.

E184.I6B89 2004
973'.049162--dc22

2003062810

Contents

Irish Americans 4
Emerald Isle 6
Land of Hope. 12
Becoming a Citizen 18
A Proud Culture. 20
Defining America. 26
Glossary 30
Saying It 31
Web Sites. 31
Index 32

Irish Americans

Christopher Columbus visited the New World in 1492. This set off a wave of European exploration. People from England, France, Spain, and the Netherlands came to start colonies. In the 1800s and 1900s, great **migrations** of people came to America's shores. They were looking for freedom and opportunity.

Many of these **immigrants** came from Ireland. They were not expecting to make a lot of money in the United States. The Irish were only hoping to survive. They came to escape **famine** and an uncertain future.

Irish Americans faced injustice and **prejudice** in America, just like other immigrants. They struggled to learn a new way of life. But, the Irish have made America richer and stronger. Through their struggles, they have taught everyone what it means to be American.

These girls celebrate before marching in a parade on Saint Patrick's Day.

Emerald Isle

Ireland is an island in the northern Atlantic Ocean. It is the subject of many songs and legends. It is sometimes called the Emerald Isle because of its many green, grassy hills. The people there share a powerful and ancient **culture**. But, Ireland has suffered centuries of war, poverty, and misery.

People have been living in Ireland for nearly 8,000 years. Waves of later civilizations crossed the ocean to Ireland from other European countries. Around 300 BC, the Celts arrived from mainland Europe. They brought with them a culture and language that shaped Irish history.

The lush, green countryside gives the Emerald Isle its name.

Actors portray Celtic warriors in a historical re-enactment. Warriors were important in Celtic society. In battle, they used large shields, swords, and spears.

Under the Celts, Ireland was divided into many small kingdoms. Around AD 400, most European countries fell into the **Dark Ages**. Ireland, however, prospered at this time. Its **monasteries** and schools retained the knowledge of Western civilization.

Ireland did not remain under Celtic rule, however. The Celts resisted forming large, powerful kingdoms or empires. This meant that the Irish often had a hard time forming armies. Their armies were not large enough to resist the many invaders who were poised to attack Ireland.

First it was the Vikings, who were Scandinavian warriors. They raided Irish towns. They ruled parts of the country until 1014. Then came the French-speaking Normans, who built towering castles and great cities.

Actors portray Viking women in Ireland as part of a re-enactment at the National Heritage Park in Ferrycarrig, Ireland.

In the mid-1500s, the king of England also became king of Ireland. For hundreds of years after that, England ruled Ireland harshly. The English seized property and turned it over to the nobles. Most of the Irish population was kept in poverty.

In 1798, some Irish were inspired by the revolutions in America and France. They **rebelled** against English rule. But, England's government crushed the Irish rebellion. In 1801, Ireland became part of the **United Kingdom**.

The Norman Cahir Castle in County Tipperary, Ireland, was built in the 1200s and restored in the 1800s.

The loss of the Irish nation was followed by disaster. In the 1840s, **blight** destroyed much of Ireland's potato crop. The devastation of the blight led to the Irish Potato **Famine**. About 1 million Irish people died of hunger. A million more fled their native land. Many came to America to search for work and food.

In the late 1800s and early 1900s, Irish people pressed for their independence from the **United Kingdom**. In 1921, Britain agreed to give Ireland some power of self-government. Most of the island became the **Republic** of Ireland. But, the northeastern portion remained a part of the United Kingdom. It is called Northern Ireland.

Violence often erupts between Protestants in Northern Ireland and Catholics in Ireland. The Protestant residents of Northern Ireland want to remain a part of the United Kingdom. The Catholics in Ireland want to reunite with Northern Ireland.

Many Irish families lost their homes during the Irish Potato Famine and lived under makeshift shelters.

This is the site of Lettergarriv, an Irish village abandoned during the Irish Potato Famine.

Land of Hope

Irish people have been coming to America even before it was a country. Some say that Irish seafarers were among the first Europeans to reach the New World. This was hundreds of years before Columbus!

In the American colonies, most people were originally from England. The second-largest group of people, however, came from Ireland. Many of them were Scotch-Irish. They had come from Scotland to Ireland in the 1600s.

Unlike most Irish, who were Catholic, the Scotch-Irish were Protestant. In Ireland, conflicts often arose between Catholics and Protestants. The Scotch-Irish came to America hoping to avoid these conflicts. Many of the Scotch-Irish settled in Pennsylvania, Virginia, and North and South Carolina.

Irish emigrants get ready to board ships to America in the 1800s.

The biggest waves of Irish **immigration** to the United States began in the 1800s. During that time, the Irish wanted to escape **famine** caused by potato **blight**. So, they began heading on boats for U.S. ports. In 1851 alone, 250,000 Irish came to America.

The Journey from Ireland to the United States

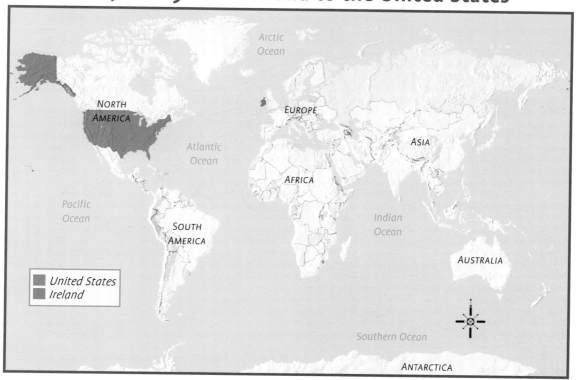

Unlike the Protestant Scotch-Irish, these new **immigrants** were Catholic. They were usually poor. And, there were many of them. For these reasons, new Irish immigrants faced fear and **discrimination** from other Americans.

Irish immigrants often lived in the worst areas of major cities such as New York and Chicago. Living in large cities was especially hard on the Irish. They were used to small villages and farms in Ireland. City life was much louder and more crowded.

Hundreds of thousands of Irish arrived in the United States during the **Civil War**. Irish soldiers fought with distinction for their new country. They helped preserve the Union and end slavery.

The Know-Nothing Party used this flyer in 1844. The party thought of its members as the only "native" Americans.

OUR COUNTRY AND HER FLAG.

NATIVE

AMERICANS.

Published & for Sale by W. L. Germon.
215 Chesnut St. 2nd door above 7th
Philadelphia.

Despite this, Irish Americans were kept out of all but low-paying jobs. Books and newspapers of the time often pictured the Irish as lazy, violent alcoholics. People who hated **immigrants** formed a political party called the Know-Nothings. They were committed to keeping the Irish and other immigrants out of the United States.

In this difficult environment, the Irish continued to struggle with **discrimination** and a lack of industrial job skills. They were forced to take dangerous jobs. Hundreds of thousands died building railroads. Some worked in coal mines. Eventually, more job opportunities opened.

The Irish immigrants of the 1800s became important to politicians who wanted many votes. Because they were numerous, the Irish Americans had growing political strength. Politicians gave them good jobs in police and fire departments.

With each generation, more Irish Americans became successful. They got better jobs and were able to send their children to college. Today, there are Irish Americans in every kind of job. They work in all career fields, from farms and factories to the White House itself.

Meanwhile, complete independence came to the **Republic** of Ireland in 1949. Northern Ireland remained under British rule. **Immigration** to the United States slowed. The sons and daughters of the Irish immigrants continued to build better lives for themselves in America.

Irish-American families grew wealthier and better educated. Irish communities spread from the big cities into suburbs and rural towns. Irish Americans began to have a major impact on American politics and **culture**. Today, Irish Americans are among the largest and most successful **ethnic** groups in the country.

This document is the Proclamation of the Irish Republic, which declared Ireland free from British rule. This brought some stability to Ireland, so emigration slowed.

POBLACHT NA H EIREANN.
THE PROVISIONAL GOVERNMENT
OF THE
IRISH REPUBLIC
TO THE PEOPLE OF IRELAND.

IRISHMEN AND IRISHWOMEN: In the name of God and of the dead generations from which she receives her old tradition of nationhood, Ireland, through us, summons her children to her flag and strikes for her freedom.

Having organised and trained her manhood through her secret revolutionary organisation, the Irish Republican Brotherhood, and through her open military organisations, the Irish Volunteers and the Irish Citizen Army, having patiently perfected her discipline, having resolutely waited for the right moment to reveal itself, she now seizes that moment, and, supported by her exiled children in America and by gallant allies in Europe, but relying in the first on her own strength, she strikes in full confidence of victory.

We declare the right of the people of Ireland to the ownership of Ireland, and to the unfettered control of Irish destinies, to be sovereign and indefeasible. The long usurpation of that right by a foreign people and government has not extinguished the right, nor can it ever be extinguished except by the destruction of the Irish people. In every generation the Irish people have asserted their right to national freedom and sovereignty; six times during the past three hundred years they have asserted it in arms. Standing on that fundamental right and again asserting it in arms in the face of the world, we hereby proclaim the Irish Republic as a Sovereign Independent State, and we pledge our lives and the lives of our comrades-in-arms to the cause of its freedom, of its welfare, and of its exaltation among the nations.

The Irish Republic is entitled to, and hereby claims, the allegiance of every Irishman and Irishwoman. The Republic guarantees religious and civil liberty, equal rights and equal opportunities to all its citizens, and declares its resolve to pursue the happiness and prosperity of the whole nation and of all its parts, cherishing all the children of the nation equally, and oblivious of the differences carefully fostered by an alien government, which have divided a minority from the majority in the past.

Until our arms have brought the opportune moment for the establishment of a permanent National Government, representative of the whole people of Ireland and elected by the suffrages of all her men and women, the Provisional Government, hereby constituted, will administer the civil and military affairs of the Republic in trust for the people.

We place the cause of the Irish Republic under the protection of the Most High God, Whose blessing we invoke upon our arms, and we pray that no one who serves that cause will dishonour it by cowardice, inhumanity, or rapine. In this supreme hour the Irish nation must, by its valour and discipline and by the readiness of its children to sacrifice themselves for the common good, prove itself worthy of the august destiny to which it is called.

Signed on Behalf of the Provisional Government,
THOMAS J. CLARKE.
SEAN Mac DIARMADA.   THOMAS MacDONAGH.
P. H. PEARSE.   EAMONN CEANNT.
JAMES CONNOLLY.   JOSEPH PLUNKETT.

Irish-American Communities

More than 100,000,000 Irish Americans	Between 250,000 and 500,000 Irish Americans	Between 50,000 and 100,000 Irish Americans
Between 500,000 and 100,000,000 Irish Americans	Between 100,000 and 250,000 Irish Americans	Fewer than 50,000 Irish Americans

Becoming a Citizen

The Irish and other **immigrants** who come to the United States take the same path to citizenship. Immigrants become citizens in a process called naturalization. A government agency called the United States Citizenship and Immigration Services (USCIS) oversees this process.

The Path to Citizenship

Applying for Citizenship

The first step in becoming a citizen is filling out a form. It is called the Application for Naturalization. On the application, immigrants provide information about their past. Immigrants send the application to the USCIS.

Providing Information

Besides the application, immigrants must provide the USCIS with other items. They may include documents such as marriage licenses or old tax returns. Immigrants must also provide photographs and fingerprints. They are used for identification. The fingerprints are also used to check whether immigrants have committed crimes in the past.

The Interview

Next, a USCIS officer interviews each immigrant to discuss his or her application and background. In addition, the USCIS officer tests the immigrant's ability to speak, read, and write in English. The officer also tests the immigrant's knowledge of American civics.

The Oath

Immigrants approved for citizenship must take the Oath of Allegiance. Once immigrants take this oath, they are citizens. During the oath, immigrants promise to renounce loyalty to their native country, to support the U.S. Constitution, and to serve and defend the United States when needed.

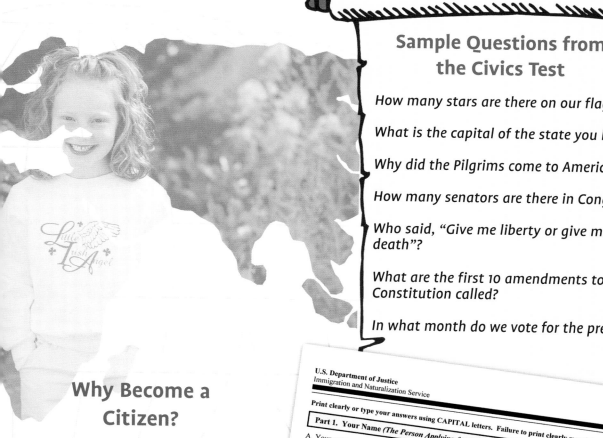

Sample Questions from the Civics Test

How many stars are there on our flag?

What is the capital of the state you live in?

Why did the Pilgrims come to America?

How many senators are there in Congress?

Who said, "Give me liberty or give me death"?

What are the first 10 amendments to the Constitution called?

In what month do we vote for the president?

Why Become a Citizen?

Why would an immigrant want to become a U.S. citizen? There are many reasons. Perhaps the biggest reason is that the U.S. Constitution grants many rights to its citizens. One of the most important is the right to vote.

U.S. Department of Justice
Immigration and Naturalization Service

Print clearly or type your answers using CAPITAL letters. Failure to print clearly may delay your application. Use b

Part 1. Your Name (The Person Applying for Naturalization)

A. Your current legal name.
Family Name (Last Name)

Given Name (First Name)

Full Middle Name (If applicable)

B. Your name exactly as it appears on your Permanent Resident Card.
Family Name (Last Name)

Given Name (First Name)

Full Middle Name (If applicable)

C. If you have ever used other names, provide them below.
Family Name (Last Name)

Given Name (First Name)

Middle Name

Application

Write your INS "A"- n
A

FOR INS U
Bar Code

A Proud Culture

Many Irish Americans have been told of the struggles their ancestors experienced in Ireland. This is one reason Irish Americans are so proud of their heritage. They celebrate their **culture** in many ways. They keep their families close, celebrate Irish holidays, and even speak the Irish language!

Family

The transition to American life was difficult for most Irish **immigrants**. One way Irish Americans tried to cope with the hardships was to keep their families close. Many Irish Americans still take comfort in the time they spend with relatives. This is a reminder of the days when family was all an Irish American had of value.

Irish Americans value time spent with their families.

Celebrate with Green!

You probably already know about the most important Irish-American celebration. It is Saint Patrick's Day, celebrated on March 17. The holiday is the feast day of Saint Patrick. He was the missionary who worked to spread Christianity in Ireland in the 400s. Today, he is the **patron saint** of Ireland.

In the United States, Irish Americans celebrate their heritage on Saint Patrick's Day. In New York, Chicago, and many other cities, Irish Americans put on parades. People wear green clothing to honor the Emerald Isle. In Chicago, they even color the Chicago River green for the day!

The Chicago River on Saint Patrick's Day

Music and Dance

Irish music and dancing is popular with Irish Americans, and with non-Irish, too! Irish dancing that features fast, high-kicking footwork has also become popular. The show Riverdance is a tribute to traditional Irish dancing. It has toured the country to packed audiences.

A traditional Irish dancer

Keeping the Faith

Many Irish Americans are members of the Catholic Church. But under British rule, the Catholic Church was outlawed. This is one of the ways that Britain controlled Ireland. However, Irish people still practiced their faith in secret. Often, this was at the risk of their lives. In the **Republic** of Ireland, being Catholic is an important part of the national identity.

Irish Americans were **discriminated** against for their religion, as well as for their nationality. But, Irish Americans held on to their faith. They built many of the first Catholic churches in the United States.

Pope John Paul II visits Saint Patrick's Cathedral in New York.

Ancient Language

English is the most common language in Ireland. Knowing English was a great advantage for the first Irish Americans. It allowed them to adjust to their new home more easily. This was not the case for many other **ethnic** groups that came to the New World.

Although many people in Ireland speak English, the country does have a more ancient language. It is called Irish Gaelic, or Irish. Irish Gaelic was brought to Ireland by the Celts about 2,000 years ago.

Almost a dead language at one point, Irish Gaelic is now making a comeback. Many people in Ireland consider learning Irish a matter of national pride. And, many Irish Americans are learning to speak it, too.

The letters in Irish Gaelic may look familiar. But, don't assume that Irish words are pronounced how they look! For instance, one way to say hello in Irish is *Dia duit*. But, would you guess that *Dia duit* is pronounced "JEE ah GITCH"? Or that the phrase for good night, *Oiche mhaith*, is pronounced "EE ha WAH"?

Opposite page: Schools that teach in Gaelic, such as this one in Ireland, help preserve the language. Many Irish Americans are also working to learn and preserve Gaelic.

Defining America

Irish **immigrants** and their descendants have made important contributions to every walk of American life. Some have become famous, although they are not known as Irish Americans. They are just Americans.

Irish Americans have played an important role at every point in the nation's history. Nellie Bly, a newspaper reporter in the 1800s, was of Irish heritage. She wrote a letter to the *Pittsburgh Dispatch* in 1885 supporting women's rights.

The editor of the paper liked her letter. He liked it so much, he offered her a job. This is how she began her career as a journalist. Later, she traveled around the world in just 72 days! She was a pioneer as an Irish American, and as a woman.

Nellie Bly's real name was Elizabeth Seaman. But, she became famous for her writing using the name Nellie Bly.

Many Irish Americans have become great political leaders. Andrew Jackson, the seventh U.S. president, was of Irish heritage. Ronald Reagan was another Irish-American president. Former president Bill Clinton is also proud of his Irish roots. He helped to promote peace in Northern Ireland.

Bill Clinton, president of the United States from 1993 to 2001, was proud of his Irish heritage. In 2000, he declared March to be Irish-American Heritage Month.

Another famous Irish-American leader was John Fitzgerald Kennedy. He was elected president in 1960. This was more than 100 years after his great-grandfather, Patrick Kennedy, arrived in America. Patrick Kennedy had traveled for one whole month to cross the Atlantic Ocean from Ireland.

Irish Americans have also become some of America's best-loved entertainers. One of the most famous is Rosie O'Donnell. Her father came to America from Belfast, Ireland. She was born in Commack, New York, and raised in an Irish Catholic family.

O'Donnell grew up to be a comedian and actress. She has starred in such movies as *Sleepless in Seattle* and *A League of Their Own*. She also hosted a talk show from 1996 to 2002. On her show, she worked to raise money for children's charities. She sets a positive example as one of the most popular Irish-American entertainers.

Today, millions of descendants of Irish **immigrants** call themselves Americans. They are so much a part of American society that some Irish Americans don't think much about their **ethnic** heritage. Each Saint Patrick's Day, however, many people still think of the home of their ancestors on the Emerald Isle with pride.

Opposite page: Rosie O'Donnell holds her Daytime Emmy Award for Outstanding Talk Show Host in 2002. She won that same award every year from 1997 to 2002!

Glossary

blight - a disease that kills plants.

civil war - a war between groups in the same country. The United States of America and the Confederate States of America fought a civil war from 1861 to 1865.

culture - the customs, arts, and tools of a nation or people at a certain time.

Dark Ages - a period in the Middle Ages (from about AD 476 to 1000) characterized by a lack of education, the loss of artistic and technical skills, population decrease, and primitive economic life.

discrimination - unfair treatment based on factors such as a person's race, religion, or gender.

ethnic - of or having to do with a group of people who are of the same race, nationality, or culture.

famine - a severe scarcity of food.

immigration - entry into another country to live. A person who immigrates is called an immigrant.

migrate - to move from one place to settle in another.

monastery - a place where monks or other members of a religious community live.

patron saint - a saint believed to be the special protector of a church, city, state, or country.

prejudice - hatred of a particular group based on factors such as race or religion.

rebel - to disobey an authority or the government.

republic - a form of government in which authority rests with voting citizens and is carried out by elected officials, such as those in a parliament.

United Kingdom - the united countries of England, Scotland, Wales, and Northern Ireland.

Saying It

blight - BLITE
Celt - KEHLT
Gaelic - GAY-lihk
Nellie Bly - NEHL-ee BLEYE

Web Sites

To learn more about Irish Americans, visit ABDO Publishing Company on the World Wide Web at **www.abdopub.com**. Web sites about Irish Americans are featured on our Book Links page. These links are routinely monitored and updated to provide the most current information available.

Index

A
Atlantic Ocean 6, 28

B
Belfast, Ireland 28
Bly, Nellie 26

C
Celts 6, 8, 24
Chicago, Illinois 14, 21
citizenship 18
Civil War, U.S. 14, 15
Clinton, Bill 27
Columbus, Christopher 4, 12
Commack, New York 28

D
dance 22
discrimination 4, 14, 15, 23

E
England 4, 9, 12

F
family 16, 20, 28
famine 4, 10, 13
France 4, 9

G
Great Britain 9, 10, 16, 23

I
Ireland, Republic of 10, 16, 23

J
Jackson, Andrew 27

K
Kennedy, John Fitzgerald 28
Kennedy, Patrick 28
Know-Nothing Party 15

L
language 6, 8, 20, 24

M
music 22

N
Netherlands, the 4
New York City, New York 14, 21
Normans 8
North Carolina 12
Northern Ireland 10, 16, 27

O
O'Donnell, Rosie 28

P
Pennsylvania 12

R
Reagan, Ronald 27
religion 10, 12, 14, 21, 23, 28

S
Saint Patrick's Day 21, 28
Scotch-Irish 12, 14
Scotland 12
South Carolina 12
Spain 4

U
United Kingdom 9, 10
United States Citizenship and Immigration Services 18

V
Vikings 8
Virginia 12